A personal prayer guide

a pattern for conversation with God

© Scripture Union 2005, compiled and edited by Lin Ball
First published 2005, reprinted 2006
ISBN 1 84427 135 8

Scripture Union, 207-209 Queensway, Bletchley, Milton Keynes, MK2 2EB, UK.

Email: info@scriptureunion.org.uk
Website: www.scriptureunion.org.uk

Scripture Union Australia
Locked Bag 2, Central Coast Business centre, NSW 2252.
Website: www.su.org.au

Scripture Union USA
PO Box 987, Valley Forge, PA 19482.
Website: www.scriptureunion.org

Quotations from the New International Version of the Holy Bible, © 1973, 1978,
1984 by International Bible Society, used by permission of Hodder and Stoughton
Limited.

British Library Cataloguing-in-Publication Data: a catalogue record for this book is
available from the British Library.

Cover design and photography by Apostle Designs
Internal design and typesetting by Donna Pendrey
Printed and bound by Henry Ling Limited, at the Dorset Press, Dorchester, DT1 1HD

Scripture Union: Scripture Union is an international Christian charity working
with churches in more than 130 countries providing resources to bring the good
news about Jesus Christ to children, young people and families – and to
encourage them to develop spiritually through the Bible and prayer. As well as a
network of volunteers, staff and associates who run holidays, church-based events
and school Christian groups, SU produces a wide range of publications and
supports those who use the resources through training programmes.

Introduction

We're all so good at excuses! True, schedules are hectic for many of us. Fast-paced contemporary lifestyles often impoverish our most important relationships with those who are dear to us, so it's hardly surprising that we find it hard to sustain intimacy with the invisible God. He is a God who has the greatest claims on us, yet is never insistent. When we do spend time getting to know him better – through prayer, meditation, reading the Bible – we are often surprised to find ourselves warmed, blessed, encouraged, affirmed; sometimes when we honestly expected reprimand or judgement. But the lessons are quickly lost as we immerse ourselves in the demands of our timetables.

We know there are good reasons why we should pray. We understand the benefits of living close to our Creator, of being in harmony with our Saviour. We realise that we have an inbuilt tendency to give priority to the urgent over the important. We appreciate the model provided in the Gospels of Jesus himself spending time with the Father. But still we find it hard; we deem it a discipline rather than a joy to pray. Fresh resolutions are short-lived. We are indeed fickle and ungrateful.

The guilt feelings may be familiar. Our disregard for prayer may have become cynically acceptable to us. But have we the commitment for just one more effort, as offered by this guide? Because there is always effort involved. It is an act of will to turn aside from the tyranny of the schedule or the demands of the family to look into the face of God and talk to him.

This slim diary has no magical qualities. It will not make your prayer life easy. It will not create time and space in your schedule that you had previously overlooked. It offers no easy steps to the experience of answered prayer. It is just a simple tool. But it may be just the help you need to give a shape or focus or framework to time with God that brings the ambition of a closer relationship with him a little nearer. It is built on the idea of using the words of Scripture itself to help us praise and thank God; to pray for ourselves, others, and our world.

There are no hard and fast rules about how to use this diary. There is no minimum time frame suggested. It's not vital to have a particular place in which to pray, although some people find that really helpful. Your preference for praying aloud or silently, praying on your knees or as you walk, in the morning or at night – these are considerations for you to explore within your knowledge of your own personality.

Don't begin it with unrealistic expectations of yourself. But do begin with the expectation that God will always be there in whatever rushed moments you are able to give him, and begin with the confidence that his loving desire is to communicate with you. Be as ready to listen as to speak. We would all live our lives with more certainty, more confidence, more energy, if we were to spend time discovering from God his purpose and call on our lives. It is his joy to give us that purpose. It is his Father's heart to guide us and just to be there for us when we need him.

Using this prayer guide

Use the pattern outlined either every time you come to God in prayer or for any opportunity you have in your week to snatch more than a few minutes of prayer. Use the words of Scripture to focus your prayers and briefly record any thoughts along the way. Often a pattern like this can help develop good habits and, as you become more familiar with it, using it thoughtfully and deliberately will become easier and more instinctive. Looking back over what you have written may well help you identify the way God is guiding you. Using the same Scripture verses over a period of a week will help you meditate on them and discover more layers of truth. But, once familiar with the pattern, don't be afraid to divert from it from time to time! Don't forget that there is always room for 'AOB' (Any Other Business) on God's agenda! Using the diary on a weekly basis will give you material for a full quarter.

❖ Come to him in praise
Use these verses to praise God:

> *I will declare that your love stands firm for ever,*
>> *that you established your faithfulness in heaven*
>>> *itself.* (Psalm 89:2)

> *You are mighty, O LORD, and your faithfulness*
>> *surrounds you.* (Psalm 89:8)

❖ Come to him in confession
Admit your own sinfulness and ask for forgiveness:

> *He who conceals his sins does not prosper,*
>> *but whoever confesses and renounces them finds*
>>> *mercy.* (Proverbs 28:13)

❖ Come to him for others
Focus on national and church leaders. Use this verse to pray for their spiritual growth:

> *...we pray this in order that you may live a life worthy of the Lord and may please him in every way: bearing fruit in every good work, growing in the knowledge of God, being strengthened with all power according to his glorious might so that you may have great endurance and patience, and joyfully giving thanks to the Father, who has qualified you to share in the inheritance of the saints in the kingdom of light.*
> (Colossians 1:10–12)

And list here any Christian leaders known to you, that they may realise their full potential in Christ:

_____

_____

_____

❖ Come to him for yourself

Pray for yourself, especially in the area of experiencing the reality of the presence of the God who speaks of his people with confident love:

> *Fear not, for I have redeemed you;*
> *   I have summoned you by name; you are mine.*
> *When you pass through the waters,*
> *   I will be with you;*
> *and when you pass through the rivers,*
> *   they will not sweep over you... (Isaiah 43:1,2)*

And write here any particular concerns or anxieties you want to share with your Father:

_____

_____

_____

❖ Listen to God

Note here any words of guidance, challenge or love you hear this week:

_____

_____

_____

❖ Thank and trust God

Confirm your confidence in God and your continuing trust in him:

> *...great are your purposes and mighty are your deeds. Your eyes are open to all the ways of men; you reward everyone according to his conduct and as his deeds deserve. (Jeremiah 32:19)*

❖ Come to him in praise

Meditate on the natural world to stir in yourself a spirit of praise:

> *You alone are the LORD. You made the heavens, even the high-est heavens, and all their starry host, the earth and all that is on it, the seas and all that is in them. You give life to every-thing, and the multitudes of heaven worship you.*
>
> (Nehemiah 9:6)

❖ Come to him in confession

Make a fresh commitment to honesty about your own shortcomings:

> *...whoever lives by the truth comes into the light...* (John 3:21)

❖ Come to him for others

Pray for Christian ministries and missionary outreach, using this blessing:

> *...may they who love you be like the sun when it rises in its strength...*   (Judges 5:31)

Note down any you know struggling with family breakdown. Pray that God will similarly bless them with his strength.

_____

_____

_____

❖ Come to him for yourself

Pray that you will experience Jesus to be the one who satisfies the needs of your heart:

> ...whoever drinks the water I give him will never thirst. Indeed, the water I give him will become in him a spring of water welling up to eternal life. (John 4:14)

And record here any area of emptiness or lack of purpose you want to offer up to God to fill:

_____

_____

_____

❖ Listen to God

Note here any words of guidance, challenge or love you hear:

_____

_____

_____

❖ Thank and trust God

Express your dependence on God:

> It is God who arms me with strength and makes my way perfect. (2 Samuel 22:33)

Week 3

❖ Come to him in praise

Praise God for his love – a love that embraces the world but also is directed at you as an individual:

> *For God so loved the world that he gave his one and only Son, that whoever believes in him shall not perish but have eternal life.* (John 3:16)

❖ Come to him in confession

Talk to the God who longs for his people to follow him closely:

> *...be careful to do what the LORD your God has commanded you; do not turn aside to the right or to the left. Walk in all the way that the LORD your God has commanded you, so that you may live and prosper and prolong your days...* (Deuteronomy 5:32,33)

❖ Come to him for others

Commit to God all schools, colleges and other places of learning and training, that they will mentor well the next generation:

> *Then you will know the truth, and the truth will set you free.* (John 8:32)

List here any known to you who are in need of grasping God's truth because they feel trapped by circumstances or unhelpful influences:

_____

_____

_____

❖ Come to him for yourself
Pray that you might know peace of mind and heart:

> *...the peace of God, which transcends all understanding, will guard your hearts and your minds in Christ Jesus.*
> (Philippians 4:7)

Jot down here any area of your life that may be disturbing your relationship with God:

_____

_____

_____

❖ Listen to God
Note here any words of guidance, challenge or love you hear this week:

_____

_____

_____

❖ Thank and trust God
Thank God for his commitment to you as expressed in many promises of the Bible:

> *You will keep in perfect peace*
> *him whose mind is steadfast,*
> *because he trusts in you.* (Isaiah 26:3)

❖ Come to him in praise
Celebrate the joy of being in relationship with God:

> *The LORD is my strength and my song;*
>   *he has become my salvation.*
> *He is my God and I will praise him...* (Exodus 15:2)

❖ Come to him in confession
Approach God in confidence about your failings:

> *...you are a forgiving God, gracious and compassionate,*
> *slow to anger and abounding in love...* (Nehemiah 9:17)

❖ Come to him for others
Pray for your family, that those who know God might know him more, and that those who are strangers to him may recognise his Shepherd's voice:

> *He tends his flock like a shepherd:*
>   *He gathers the lambs in his arms*
> *and carries them close to his heart;*
>   *he gently leads those that have young.*
>   (Isaiah 40:11)

Name here any you know who are struggling with issues of redundancy or disappointment in the workplace, that they might experience the Shepherd's guidance and provision:

_____

_____

_____

❖ Come to him for yourself
Ask God to help you grow in intimacy with him:

> *I am the vine; you are the branches. If a man remains in me and I in him, he will bear much fruit; apart from me you can do nothing.* (John 15:5)

Record any fears you have about the future and pray to know God's security:

_____

_____

_____

❖ Listen to God
Note here any words of guidance, challenge or love you hear this week:

_____

_____

_____

❖ Thank and trust God
Confirm your dependence on God above all others:

> *Acknowledge and take to heart this day that the Lord is God in heaven above and on the earth below. There is no other.* (Deuteronomy 4:39)

❖ Come to him in praise
Give God praise for his faithfulness:

> ...there is no God like you in heaven or on earth – you who
> keep your covenant of love with your servants who continue
> wholeheartedly in your way.   (2 Chronicles 6:14)

❖ Come to him in confession
Be real with God about the condition of your heart and receive his forgiveness:

> The heart is deceitful above all things
>   and beyond cure.
> Who can understand it? (Jeremiah 17:9)

❖ Come to him for others
Pray for your church family to follow God with persistence and for those who encourage and disciple them:

> In all my prayers for all of you, I always pray with joy because
> of your partnership in the gospel...being confident...that he
> who began a good work in you will carry it on to completion...
>   (Philippians 1:4–6)

Make a prayerful note of any church members who are experiencing loss of confidence in their faith:

_____

_____

_____

❖ Come to him for yourself

Pray that God will equip you for present and future testing times:

> *…you know that the testing of your faith develops*
> *perseverance.* (James 1:3)

Describe in a few words any current struggle which is hampering your spiritual growth:

_____

_____

_____

❖ Listen to God

Note here any words of guidance, challenge or love you hear this week:

_____

_____

_____

❖ Thank and trust God

Rejoice that God is with you:

> *…surely I am with you always, to the very end of the age.*
> (Matthew 28:20)

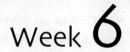

❖ Come to him in praise

Take courage from the reliability of God and praise him for his strength:

> *The LORD is my rock, my fortress and my deliverer;*
> *my God is my rock, in whom I take refuge,*
> *my shield and the horn of my salvation.*
> *He is my stronghold, my refuge and my saviour...*
> (2 Samuel 22:2,3)

❖ Come to him in confession

Be as ready to ask forgiveness as he is to forgive:

> *Those whom I love I rebuke and discipline. So be earnest, and repent. Here I am! I stand at the door and knock...*
> (Revelation 3:19,20)

❖ Come to him for others

Pray for all around the world who are in situations of war and unrest and for politicians, aid workers and others who wrestle with finding solutions:

> *Peacemakers who sow in peace raise a harvest of righteousness.*
> (James 3:18)

Ask God to bring peace into the lives of any you know here who live in situations of family hostility or stressed relationships. Make a note of them below:

_____

_____

_____

❖ Come to him for yourself

Commit yourself, with God's help, to speaking words of peace and reconciliation into difficult relationships around you:

> *I am not ashamed of the gospel, because it is the power of God for the salvation of everyone who believes...* (Romans 1:16)

List situations you are aware of that will require God-given courage from you to address:

_____

_____

_____

❖ Listen to God

Note here any words of guidance, challenge or love you hear this week:

_____

_____

_____

❖ Thank and trust God

Trust in God to enable you to speak out and live for him:

> *...the Counsellor, the Holy Spirit, whom the Father will send in my name, will teach you all things and will remind you of everything I have said to you.* (John 14:26)

❖ Come to him in praise

Praise God for all that he has done in your life so far:

> *Great and marvellous are your deeds,*
> *Lord God Almighty.*
> *Just and true are your ways,*
> *King of the ages.* (Revelation 15:3)

❖ Come to him in confession

Pray for greater awareness of the potential for temptation in your daily life:

> *Be self-controlled and alert. Your enemy the devil prowls around*
> *like a roaring lion looking for someone to devour. Resist him,*
> *standing firm in the faith...* (1 Peter 5:8,9)

❖ Come to him for others

Ask God to bring about mercy for the vulnerable in our society:

> *I know that the LORD secures justice for the poor*
> *and upholds the cause of the needy.*
> (Psalm 140:12)

Name and pray for the elderly members of your own and your church family; for the children you are closest to; and for anyone else you feel to be in a situation of vulnerability:

_____

_____

_____

❖ Come to him for yourself

Pray that you will become more Christ-like in your relationships with others:

> Do nothing out of selfish ambition or vain conceit, but in humility consider others better than yourselves...look not only to your own interests, but also to the interests of others.
> (Philippians 2:3,4)

Pray particularly for any you find it hard to get on with, and ask God for his grace in those relationships:

_____

_____

_____

❖ Listen to God

Note here any words of guidance, challenge or love you hear this week:

_____

_____

_____

❖ Thank and trust God

Affirm your dependence on God to fulfil your potential as his servant:

> May the God of hope fill you with all joy and peace as you trust in him, so that you may overflow with hope by the power of the Holy Spirit.
> (Romans 15:13)

❖ Come to him in praise

Express your gratitude to God for the great gift of salvation:

*Salvation is found in no-one else, for there is no other name
under heaven given to men by which we must be saved.*
(Acts 4:12)

❖ Come to him in confession

Ask for God's wisdom to make right decisions:

*...Light has come into the world, but men loved darkness
instead of life because their deeds were evil.* (John 3:19)

❖ Come to him for others

Pray for Christians working in caring professions such as hospitals
and nursing homes, particularly as they face difficult ethical issues:

*I keep asking that the God of our Lord Jesus Christ, the glorious
Father, may give you the Spirit of wisdom and revelation, so
that you may know him better. I pray also that the eyes of your
heart may be enlightened...* (Ephesians 1:17,18)

Ask God to give wisdom to any you know working in science and
medicine:

_____

_____

_____

❖ Come to him for yourself

Call on God's protection for your body, mind and spirit:

> *For he will command his angels concerning you*
> *to guard you in all your ways;*
> *they will lift you up in their hands,*
> *so that you will not strike your foot against a*
> *stone.* (Psalm 91:11)

Write down and pray about any area of your life in which you feel weak at the moment:

_____

_____

_____

❖ Listen to God

Note here any words of guidance, challenge or love you hear this week:

_____

_____

_____

❖ Thank and trust God

Thank God for the security of belonging to him – now and for eternity:

> *...God's solid foundation stands firm, sealed with this*
> *inscription: 'The Lord knows those who are his'...*
> (2 Timothy 2:19)

❖ Come to him in praise

Tell God how important he is in your life, how central to your affections and motivations:

> O LORD, you are my God;
>   I will exalt you and praise your name,
> for in perfect faithfulness
>   you have done marvellous things,
>   things planned long ago. (Isaiah 25:1)

❖ Come to him in confession

Make a commitment to actively choosing God's way every day:

> Submit yourselves, then, to God. Resist the devil, and he will
> flee from you.   (James 4:7)

❖ Come to him for others

Ask for Christians to be people of prayer and repentance, bringing about healing of their communities, just as God promised Solomon at the dedication of the new Temple:

> ...if my people, who are called by my name, will humble them-
> selves and pray and seek my face and turn from their wicked
> ways, then will I hear from heaven and will forgive their sin and
> will heal their land.   (2 Chronicles 7:14)

Pray for churches in your locality by name:

_____

_____

_____

❖ Come to him for yourself
Re-commit yourself to aligning your whole life on godly principles:

> *Your word is a lamp to my feet*
> *and a light for my path.* (Psalm 119:105)

Pray about any lifestyle issues in which you may be more in tune with the world than with the Word:

_____

_____

_____

❖ Listen to God
Note here any words of guidance, challenge or love you hear this week:

_____

_____

_____

❖ Thank and trust God
Be thankful that he is not a distant God, but one who draws near:

> *This is the confidence we have in approaching God: that if we*
> *ask anything according to his will, he hears us.* (1 John 5:14)

❖ Come to him in praise

Express your wonder at God's wisdom:

> *Oh, the depths of the riches of the*
> *wisdom and knowledge of God!*
> *How unsearchable his judgements,*
> *and his paths beyond tracing out!*
> (Romans 11:33)

❖ Come to him in confession

Check out how closely you are following God's laws:

> *Observe the commands of the LORD your God, walking in his*
> *ways and revering him.* (Deuteronomy 8:6)

❖ Come to him for others

Pray for all Christians in the public eye, in whatever field, that they may 'shine like stars' for their faith:

> *Do everything without complaining or arguing, so that you may*
> *become blameless and pure, children of God without fault in a*
> *crooked and depraved generation, in which you shine like stars*
> *in the universe as you hold out the word of life...*
> (Philippians 2:14–16)

Pray by name for Christians in your locality or in your profession who have demanding roles, and for Christians in the media:

_____

_____

_____

❖ Come to him for yourself

Ask for courage to seize the 'everything' for your life that Peter says we have through knowing Jesus:

> *His divine power has given us everything we need for life and godliness through our knowledge of him who called us by his own glory and goodness.* (2 Peter 1:3)

Pray about any lack of courage or other obstacles which prevent you from 'shining like stars' in the areas of life in which you have influence:

_____

_____

_____

❖ Listen to God

Note here any words of guidance, challenge or love you hear this week:

_____

_____

_____

❖ Thank and trust God

Seek to have a positive attitude that is based on your sense of security in your loving Father:

> *Be joyful always; pray continually; give thanks in all circumstances, for this is God's will for you in Christ Jesus.* (1 Thessalonians 5:16–18)

❖ Come to him in praise

See yourself as just one small voice in the immense praise given to
God by the whole of creation:

> *Let everything that has breath praise the LORD...*
> (Psalm 150:6)

❖ Come to him in confession

Ask God to help you be more in tune with him and less susceptible
to temptation:

> *Forgive us our sins, for we also forgive everyone who sins*
> *against us. And lead us not into temptation.* (Luke 11:4)

❖ Come to him for others

Pray that God will enable and equip his people to achieve great
things for the Kingdom:

> *Each one should use whatever gift he has received to serve*
> *others, faithfully administering God's grace in its various forms.*
> (1 Peter 4:10)

List here and pray for two or three Christians in your church who
you would like to see grow in their gifting from God, and use their
talents to benefit the Kingdom:

_____

_____

_____

❖ Come to him for yourself

Ask God to grow you in ways that will make you a more useful servant to him:

> ...God did not give us a spirit of timidity, but a spirit of power, of love and of self-discipline. (2 Timothy 1:7)

Consider what gifting would better equip you to witness for Christ:

_____

_____

_____

❖ Listen to God

Note here any words of guidance, challenge or love you hear this week:

_____

_____

_____

❖ Thank and trust God

With thankfulness, take the example of Jesus into your day:

> Let us fix our eyes on Jesus, the author and perfecter of our faith, who for the joy set before him endured the cross, scorning its shame, and sat down at the right hand of the throne of God. (Hebrews 12:2)

❖ Come to him in praise
Rejoice in God's love for you:

> *This is love: not that we loved God, but that he loved us and sent his Son as an atoning sacrifice for our sins.* (1 John 4:10)

❖ Come to him in confession
Claim God's promise to remove all your sin and remember it no more:

> *If you, O LORD, kept a record of sins,*
> *O LORD, who could stand?*
> *But with you there is forgiveness...* (Psalm 130:3,4)

❖ Come to him for others
Pray that those most in need of our compassion will receive all that they need:

> *The LORD watches over the alien*
> *and sustains the fatherless and the widow...*
> (Psalm 146:9)

Ask God to bless and provide for any you know personally who seem unjustly treated or in particular need of support:

_____

_____

_____

❖ Come to him for yourself
Release all your worries into the hands of the Father who loves you more than anyone else:

Cast all your anxiety on him because he cares for you.
(1 Peter 5:7)

List here any special concerns that you want to hand over to God:

_____

_____

_____

❖ Listen to God
Note here any words of guidance, challenge or love you hear this week:

_____

_____

_____

❖ Thank and trust God
Be glad in the never-ending nature of God's love:

Because of the LORD's great love we are not consumed,
for his compassions never fail.
They are new every morning;
great is your faithfulness. (Lamentations 3:22,23)

❖ Come to him in praise
Celebrate the difference that knowing God has made in your life:

> *You are my lamp, O LORD;*
> *the LORD turns my darkness into light.*
> (2 Samuel 22:29)

❖ Come to him in confession
Ask God for cleansing – and praise him for the future reward of following in his ways:

> *Blessed are those who wash their robes, that they may have the right to the tree of life and may go through the gates into the city.* (Revelation 22:14)

❖ Come to him for others
Pray for a world spoiled by disease and famine, and for medical and relief personnel working with those who are suffering:

> *...the prayer offered in faith will make the sick person well; the Lord will raise him up...* (James 5:15)

Ask God to touch and encourage any known to you who are struggling with chronic physical or mental illness or disability:

_____

_____

_____

❖ Come to him for yourself

Pray that you will experience God's healing – body, mind and spirit:

Praise the LORD, O my soul,
    and forget not all his benefits –
who forgives all your sins
    and heals all your diseases,
who redeems your life from the pit
    and crowns you with love and compassion...
                              (Psalm 103:2–4)

Commit to God any needs for healing you know remain in your life:

_____

_____

_____

❖ Listen to God

Note here any words of guidance, challenge or love you hear this week:

_____

_____

_____

❖ Thank and trust God

Express your confidence in the total power of the God you serve:

Now to him who is able to do immeasurably more than all we ask or imagine, according to his power that is at work within us, to him be glory in the church and in Christ Jesus throughout all generations, for ever and ever! Amen. (Ephesians 3:20,21)

Other prayer resources from Scripture Union

How to Pray When Life Hurts: a practical book about prayer during times of illness or bereavement, guilt, anxiety, fear or anger.

A Journey of the Heart: Six Bible-based studies to help you on your own or in a group to pray with purpose and grow in intimacy with God.

Multi-Sensory Prayer: Over 60 innovative ideas to help you meet God in active prayer! Ideal for home groups and services.

Multi-Sensory Church: meditations, liturgical prayers, interactive labyrinths and prayer installations to transform your church service into a multi-sensory experience.

The Lost Art of Meditation: Explore creative, two-way communication with the amazing God of the universe.

Healing the Wounded Heart: an inspiring personal study journal to nurture spiritual health and growth.

Dangerous Praying: drawing on Ephesians, this book is packed with practical ideas and strategies to help develop a dynamic prayer life, either individually or in a group.

Ready to Grow: For Christians looking for fresh approaches to their walk with God, to Bible reading and prayer. Not just for the beginner.

SU also produces Bible reading notes for children, teens and young adults.

For details:
- visit your local Christian bookshop
- phone SU's mail order line: 0845 0706 006
- email info@scriptureunion.org.uk
- fax 01908 856020
- log on to www.scriptureunion.org.uk
- write to SU Mail Order, PO Box 5148, Milton Keynes MLO, MK2 2YX